27 Short Plays About Being Murdered in a Hotel by ABBA

a play

by William M. Razavi

MALCONTENT BOOKS
TEXAS

27 Short Plays About Being Murdered in a Hotel by ABBA

a play

by William M. Razavi

MALCONTENT BOOKS

TEXAS

27 Short Plays About Being Murdered in a Hotel by ABBA
Copyright © 2015 by William M. Razavi

ISBN-13: 978-1514193877
ISBN-10: 1514193876

Malcontent Books
Helotes, Texas

Table of Contents

27 Short Plays About Being Murdered in a Hotel by ABBA

a play

by William M. Razavi

MALCONTENT BOOKS
TEXAS

27 Short Plays About Being Murdered in a Hotel by ABBA was first produced at the Overtime Theater in San Antonio, Texas on 10 July 2015. The production was directed by William M. Razavi.

Asta	Morgan Clyde
Greta	Vanessa Eichler
Anni-Frid (Frida)	Sarah Perkins
Agnetha	Laura Epstein
Benny	Ty Mylnar
Bjorn	Nathan Thurman
Guinevere/The Pigeon/	
Dancer 1/Tomoe/Lena	
Margot	Abbey Storch
Brandon/Not Fernando/	
The Retainer/Matamoros/	
Hubert	Colin Bonnington
Ashleigh/Bartender/Narrator/	
Ramona	Cristina Vazquez
Johan/Jimmy/Dancer 2/	
Henry/Septimus/Werther/	
Fernando/The Captain	Venny Mortimer
Fran/Sybil/Death	Michele Wisniewski
Hubler/The Cook/	
Tony Romo	Dyandra Edwards
The Abbaphobe	Deborah Basham-Burns

27 Short Plays About Being Murdered in a Hotel by ABBA
a play
by William M. Razavi

The stage should have some rudimentary features of several spaces in a hotel. The central feature is a hotel room with a bed, an exit to a balcony and perhaps a door leading to the bathroom. There is also something to represent a hotel bar/restaurant, which can also double as the concierge desk/lobby. The exit to the balcony can be doubled as the elevator or the elevator can be represented as a square of light. (N.B. The original production also featured a section of floor painted in a black and white checkerboard pattern.)

1. GIMME A MAN AFTER MIDNIGHT

A hotel room. A man and a woman enter.

BRANDON: This is it.

ASHLEIGH: Nice room.

BRANDON: Yeah.

ASHLEIGH: It's pretty much like my room.

BRANDON: Yeah.

ASHLEIGH: I wonder if we have the same view.

BRANDON: I don't know.

They stand around awkwardly for a moment, then begin making out furiously.

ASHLEIGH: I really like you.

BRANDON: Yeah, I like you too.

They make out some more.

ASHLEIGH: This is really crazy. I've never met someone when I'm on vacation before.

BRANDON: Yeah. It's crazy.

They continue making out.

ASHLEIGH: Say something dirty.

BRANDON: What?

ASHLEIGH: I want to be dirty.

BRANDON: Okay.

ASHLEIGH: Don't you want to be dirty?

BRANDON: Sure.

ASHLEIGH: Say something. Talk dirty to me.

BRANDON: Okay, um…I'm gonna stick my finger in your ass and then I'm gonna lick it.

Ashleigh breaks off from him immediately.

ASHLEIGH: What the fuck?

BRANDON: What?

ASHLEIGH: You can't just do that without asking permission.

BRANDON: I didn't do it yet.

ASHLEIGH: Oh, but you were planning on doing it?

BRANDON: What?

ASHLEIGH: Do you have a vocabulary or are you just a stupid dick that says 'what'?

BRANDON: What?

ASHLEIGH: You think you can just stick your finger in someone's ass just like that? Why is that even the first thing that came to your mind?

BRANDON: You told me to talk dirty. I thought that was pretty dirty.

ASHLEIGH: And exactly what were you going to lick?

BRANDON: What?

ASHLEIGH: Seriously. Learn to keep up with the conversation.

BRANDON: What?

ASHLEIGH: Fuck, you're a stupid nutbag. What were you going to lick, your finger or my ass?

BRANDON: I don't know.

ASHLEIGH: Here's a clue. Next time you have a stupid thing to say, just don't say it. I'm going to my room. Buy yourself a dictionary and stop watching porn.

Ashleigh moves to the door. Brandon immediately blocks her way.

ASHLEIGH: Get out of my way. I'm leaving.

BRANDON: You have to give me something before you go.

ASHLEIGH: Fuck you. Step aside so I can go.

BRANDON: Fuck it, I'm bigger than you. What do you think you can do? We're gonna finish this, then you can go.

ASHLEIGH: What the fuck?

BRANDON: Something like that.

ASHLEIGH: Something like what?

BRANDON: Fucking.

ASHLEIGH: Get away from the door.

BRANDON: Only if you give me something I want.

Brandon moves toward Ashleigh who backs away from the door. There's a flash of light. The curtain of the balcony window opens to reveal four people standing. It's ABBA, aka Anni-Frid, Benny, Björn and Agnetha. They are each armed with some sort of cutting or bludgeoning implement. They are at first unnoticed by Brandon and Ashleigh as she retreats in the direction of the bed and he stalks her. Another flash of light. Music. Now Brandon and Ashleigh notice the presence of ABBA.

BRANDON: What the fuck?

Music continues. Benny and Björn chase down Brandon and one of them manages to strike Brandon in the head. Benny and Agnetha restrain Brandon while Björn and Anni-Frid each take a turn stabbing him. Brandon falls to the ground behind the bed. ABBA stands around him clearly administering a savage kicking to Brandon, who tries to get up and crawl on the bed only to be dragged back and smacked around until he falls back down behind the bed. Ashleigh is frozen in a combination of terror and relief. This process continues for an uncomfortably long time. Finally, the music fades out and it is clear there is nothing left of Brandon behind the bed.

ASHLEIGH: Thank you. You saved me.

Anni-Frid walks up to Ashleigh with a gentle smile on her face. There is a moment where it looks like they will hug, but Anni-Frid stabs Ashleigh in the abdomen.

ASHLEIGH: What the fuck? Why?

Blackout.

2. TEARS OF A CLOWN

Lights. The hotel room again. Laid out on the head of the bed is a big red clown wig. At the foot of the bed there is a pair of clown shoes. In between is a large pair of clown pants and red nose. A pair of detectives is looking around. Asta, a detective dressed in punk-ish/goth-ish style with various piercings and tattoos, takes the lead looking around the hotel room. Greta, a detective dressed in plainer clothes, hangs back eating some Toblerone chocolate.

ASTA: What we have here is a dead clown.

GRETA: That's exactly what we don't have. We have remnants of clown matter. But where's the clown?

Asta discovers a large jar or a plastic tub that is filled with some sort of horrific brownish red smoothie. It has the word "CLOWN" written on a piece of paper taped to it.

ASTA: Here's the clown.

GRETA: How do you know that's the clown?

Asta points out the writing.

GRETA: That doesn't prove anything. You can't assume these things.

Asta opens the lid of the container and gets a horrific whiff of the dead clown smoothie.

ASTA: Yeah, that's the clown.

GRETA: Who would want to liquefy a clown?

ASTA: Did you take that Toblerone from the minibar?

GRETA: No.

ASTA: You didn't have it a minute ago.

GRETA: It's not like that clown is going to miss it.

ASTA: That's not the point. We're here to solve a crime not to commit crimes.

GRETA: It's a minibar. Why do you have to be so uptight?

ASTA: It's evidence.

GRETA: No, the peanuts were evidence and I didn't touch those.

ASTA: Why would uneaten peanuts be evidence?

GRETA: Because this guy was a clown. Clowns love peanuts. Everybody knows that.

ASTA: Maybe he didn't want to pay the minibar price for peanuts.

GRETA: A clown checks into a hotel. He doesn't even bring a change of clothes. That's already strange. What kind of clown is always dressed as a clown?

ASTA: A sad clown. A poor clown.
A mentally disturbed clown.
A lonely, impoverished and quite insane clown.

GRETA: Let's say our clown was one or all of these things. He checks into a hotel room. And our sad, lonely clown isn't going to be sad and lonely enough to binge on some vodka and peanuts from a minibar?

ASTA: So what does that mean? Maybe we have a sober and happy clown.

GRETA: You and I both know that's impossible.

ASTA: Maybe we have a clown with a peanut allergy.

GRETA: Unlikely. He never would have gotten through clown college with that condition.

ASTA: Maybe he was an uneducated clown.

GRETA: You can't be a clown in this country without a clown license.

ASTA: Maybe he wasn't a real clown.

GRETA: There's no such thing as pretending to be a clown. Once you put on the big shoes and the red nose you become the thing you look like. No, this clown was a real clown and like all real clowns this one had a lot of enemies. One of those enemies finally caught up to him here.

ASTA: And they killed him and turned him into this without anyone hearing a thing?

GRETA: There was a big dance party on this floor in three of the neighboring rooms. College kids.

ASTA: Clown college?

GRETA: Regular human college.

ASTA: And none of them heard a thing?

GRETA: It wasn't a smooth jazz dance party.

ASTA: But even then, our killer—

GRETA: Or, killers.

ASTA: Our killer or killers would have had to move quickly.

GRETA: So quickly that our clown never had a chance to go for the overpriced peanuts.

ASTA: And they would have had to work quietly.

GRETA: The dance party helped cover the noise, plus three rooms full of drunk people makes for terrible witnesses.

ASTA: They sure cleaned up the place nicely.

GRETA: You noticed that too?

ASTA: You have a clown in a jar. Where's the blood-spattered bed? Where's the stained bathtub full of bone chips and bits of tissue?

GRETA: What we have here is a serious professional. This wasn't the first victim. And with that kind of speed, silence and daintiness, this is a killer who will kill again. And maybe next time it won't be just a clown.

ASTA: Is there any more of that Toblerone?

GRETA: You can have the rest of this.

Blackout.

3. JOHAN DIES AT THE END

The hotel room. ABBA are sitting around the room casually. As much as possible the band members do not look at each other but instead speak to each other while one is in profile and the other looks straight out, or various variations of such arrangements with two or more of them speaking at weird angles. This is especially true if they are standing.

ANNI-FRID: Clowns.

BENNY: No more clowns. I'm sick of killing clowns.

BJORN: Benny's right. No more clowns.

AGNETHA: We should kill with more purpose. You shouldn't have killed that girl who was trying to get away, Frida.

ANNI-FRID: We can't leave behind witnesses. Are there any more peanuts? I can't get enough of the peanuts.

BJORN: No more clowns. And Agnetha's right. You shouldn't have killed the girl. We saved her. We could have been heroes.

ANNI-FRID: We could have saved those three girls in Bratislava, too, but we chopped them into tiny little bits with machetes until our hands ached and then fed the bits to their boyfriends before we killed them. That was your idea, if I remember it right. Since when did this become about delivering justice?

BJORN: Since we started killing clowns and politicians. Imagine if we were some sort of spirit of justice and fairness that people could invoke when they're being oppressed or hurt.

ANNI-FRID: That's a stupid idea. We're not killers of evil and we're not evil killers. We're just killers. We are like death itself.

BENNY: Have you been reading German philosophy books again?

ANNI-FRID: No, I've been reading Anne of Green Gables and the newspaper.

AGNETHA: We don't have to kill for justice. I think it would just be nice if we had some running ideas. Like we could kill people who wear orange pants for a week.

ANNI-FRID: So what's wrong with killing clowns?

AGNETHA: It's just boring. And they all smell like vodka and peanuts.

BENNY: No more clowns.

BJORN: Maybe we can have some running themes like Agnetha suggested.

AGNETHA: I'm glad someone was listening.

BENNY: We could try vampirism. Or cannibalism.

ANNI-FRID: We don't need ideas. The only idea is death. Is there any Toblerone left in the minibar?

AGNETHA: I had half of it, but you can have the other half.

ANNI-FRID: Thank you.

BJORN: The real question is who *are* we?

BENNY: Have *you* been reading those German philosophy books?

AGNETHA: We are what we are. Isn't that beautiful enough?

ANNI-FRID: We are what we do.

BENNY: We are. That's all we can know. We're here.

BJORN: That's not enough for me.

ANNI-FRID: Nothing's ever enough for you. Have some chocolate and a drink.

The door opens. Johan, a traveler carrying a bag and perhaps wearing orange pants, enters and is immediately startled by the presence of ABBA.

JOHAN: I'm sorry. I must have the wrong room.

AGNETHA: No, honey. You're in the right room tonight.

Blackout. Music.

4. THE GRATUITOUS RANDY

The bar of the hotel. There is a box with what looks like a pair of legs in black pants sticking out of it. Greta looks around at the box while Asta comforts a distraught woman in a sparkly outfit who is named The Generous Guinevere.

GUINEVERE: I still can't believe he's dead.

GRETA: Well, you'd better believe it, because he's definitely dead.

GUINEVERE: He was so full of life.

ASTA: I'm sure he was...very...full of life.

GUINEVERE: I just don't understand who would do this to him.

ASTA: That's what I was about to get to. Did he have any enemies? People who might have wanted to do him harm? Ex business partners, ex lovers, rival magicians—

GRETA: Illusionists. He was an illusionist.

GUINEVERE: The Gratuitous Randy was the kindest man on the face of the earth. He was very well respected in his field. Everybody loved him.

GRETA: Obviously not everybody.

ASTA: My associate is right. Somebody must have disliked him enough to saw him in half.

GRETA: And then make his head disappear.

GUINEVERE: It's terrible.

ASTA: Speaking of which, I don't suppose you have an idea where the head could be?

GUINEVERE: No. It's just disappeared. It was his last illusion.

GRETA: That's a pretty shitty illusion.

ASTA: And you are sure this is the body of The Gratuitous Randy?

GUINEVERE: I'd recognize every part of him. I loved him and I'm very observant about small physical details. I really liked the back of his knees. They were unique.

ASTA: How long were you and The Gratuitous Randy together?

GUINEVERE: We worked together for seven years.

ASTA: Were you dating the entire time?

GRETA: They only got together about a year ago.

GUINEVERE: That's right. How did you know that?

GRETA: I'm also very observant.

ASTA: And you two never had any problems? There weren't any ex-Mrs. Gratuitous Randys out there?

GUINEVERE: No, not that he ever talked about. The Gratuitous Randy was very shy. He wasn't like some of those more flamboyant overconfident illusionists like The Flamboyant Fred or The Overconfident Wesley.
Randy was sweet. I don't know what I'll do without him.

I may have to move back to Rockville, Peoria or somewhere worse like Chicago.

Guinevere breaks down in tears.

GUINEVERE: I don't want to move to Chicago.

GRETA: Nobody should have to move to Chicago.

ASTA: Would you like some chocolate?

GUINEVERE: No thanks. I have enough chocolate. We always kept a big supply of Toblerone backstage. It was our favorite. That chocolate was what finally brought The Gratuitous Randy out of his shell and brought us together. He really loved nougat.

ASTA: That's a really sweet story.

GUINEVERE: I know. That's how I'd like to remember The Gratuitous Randy: sweet...and with a head.

ASTA: I understand. Thank you for your time Miss...do you have a last name?

GUINEVERE: It's just The Generous Guinevere.

ASTA: Well, thanks for your time, Generous Guinevere.

GRETA: We'll keep you updated on our progress.

GUINEVERE: You'll let me know if you find his head?

ASTA: You'll be the first one we call.

GUINEVERE: Thank you.

ASTA: Do you know who his next of kin is?

GRETA: For handing over the body. Well, most of the body.

GUINEVERE: That would be his mother, The Supercilious Catharine. His father, The Dormant Cornelius died when he was young.

GRETA: Do you mean when Randy was young or when the father was young?

GUINEVERE: They were both younger than they would be now.

ASTA: And both more alive than they are now.

GUINEVERE: I know. It's tragic. I'll probably never perform again.

ASTA: Give yourself time. You're still young.

GUINEVERE: I don't feel young anymore.

Silence. She looks at Asta and Greta. They nod understandingly. Music. Lights fade out.

5. EVIL SCIENTISTS LOVE A HOTEL

The hotel room. Fran, an evil scientist, and Hubler, an assistant are working with some liquid items and various tubes and flasks.

FRAN: Hubler, get me the geflageflugen!

HUBLER: Okay.

Hubler hands the geflageflugen to Fran.

FRAN: Not that one. The other geflageflugen.

HUBLER: We didn't pack the other geflageflugen, Fran.

FRAN: How am I supposed to work without the right geflageflugen? This is intolerable!
Get me a Dr. Pepper, Hubler!

HUBLER: Okay.

FRAN: Not from the minibar!

HUBLER: Okay.

Hubler opens the door. Bjorn is standing in the doorway holding a Dr. Pepper. He hands the Dr. Pepper to Hubler.

HUBLER: Thanks.

Hubler takes the Dr. Pepper to Fran who opens it up and takes a sip.

FRAN: You know what I love about hotels, Hubler?

HUBLER: Is it that you can take a dump in the bed and you

don't have to worry about cleaning it up yourself?

FRAN: No.

HUBLER: Is it the minibar?

FRAN: No.

HUBLER: Is it that there's no homeowner's association to complain about the smell coming from your laboratory?

FRAN: Yes, but that's not exactly what I was thinking.
I love the familiar unfamiliarity of hotel rooms.
Everything is almost the same no matter where you go, but it's never the same.

HUBLER: Unless you get the same room at the same hotel more than once.

FRAN: Yes, Hubler. Thanks for ruining a perfectly good bit of profundity.

HUBLER: So, what are we making? Is it a death ray?

FRAN: Hubler, did you suffer a severe head injury in your childhood?

HUBLER: Yes. How did you know?

FRAN: Lucky guess. You can't make a death ray out of liquids.

HUBLER: Not even if we go out of state?

Fran looks at Hubler for a second and ponders the meanings of the question.

FRAN: I'm just going to assume that you didn't think through the theoretical implications of that question.

HUBLER: I just thought that under the right conditions we could change the state of the fluids from liquid to something else.

FRAN: Your unpredictable intellect really frightens me.

HUBLER: Thanks. So are we making a death beverage?

FRAN: No. What we're making here is a treatment for clothing that accelerates the rate of wear so that the fabric falls apart within a few weeks.

HUBLER: That's seems pretty useless, unless you're going to sell it to clothing manufacturers so that they can make clothes that become obsolete in a matter of a few weeks.

Fran smiles broadly and nods ecstatically.

HUBLER: That's pretty evil.

FRAN: That's why we're evil scientists. Well, that's why I'm an evil scientist and you're my assistant.
And when we're done with this treatment we're going to be rich evil scientists.
Well, I'm going to be rich and some of that wealth will eventually trickle down to you.

HUBLER: I thought science was about making things better through progress.

FRAN: That's just what we tell children and people with a childlike sense of wonder. We're using science to make the economy better through the creation of wealth for people who make things for other people.

And that's the only progress that really matters.
Get me another Dr. Pepper, Hubler.

HUBLER: Okay.

*Hubler goes to the door, opens the door and finds Agnetha
standing there with a Dr. Pepper.
Hubler takes the Dr. Pepper.*

HUBLER: Thanks.

Hubler takes the Dr. Pepper to Fran.

FRAN: Do you know what's better than an ice cold Dr.
Pepper, Hubler?

HUBLER: No.

FRAN: Lots of money squeezed from the wretched dupes of
the world, that's what's better. Imagine the kind of money
we can make if we can apply this same formula to iPhones
and tablet computing devices. They'll fall apart before they
even have a chance to go obsolete the normal way.

HUBLER: But what if the formula comes into contact with
human skin, or if it's ingested.

FRAN: Why would anyone eat an iPhone?

Pause.

FRAN: Make sure we use some of our money to invest in
the health care industry. We'll have to buy some
dermatologists.

HUBLER: You can buy dermatologists?

FRAN: With the kind of money we're going to make you can buy the entire House of Representatives twice over and have enough left to buy the Senate. This Dr. Pepper tastes funny. Try it, Hubler.

HUBLER: Is that a good idea?

FRAN: Probably not.

HUBLER: Okay.

Hubler tries some of the Dr. Pepper and falls to the ground and dies after some twitching.

FRAN: That's what I thought.

Fran falls to the ground and dies. Lights.

6. TEQUILA SUNSET

The hotel bar/restaurant. The bartender keeps busy behind the bar. Asta and Greta sit at a table nursing some drinks.

ASTA: Strictly speaking we shouldn't be drinking on duty.

GRETA: Strictly speaking we shouldn't be on duty twenty-four hours a day.

ASTA: We should be drinking grasshoppers. I've never had a grasshopper. Is that tequila?

GRETA: Yes, it's tequila.

ASTA: You shouldn't sip tequila. That's a rule.

GRETA: I don't like rules.

ASTA: Rules are important. Without rules you can't define things. And if you can't define things then you can't understand things.

GRETA: Then you can define me as someone who likes to sip tequila.

ASTA: That's just now how it's done.

GRETA: It's how I do it.

ASTA: You're doing it wrong. Nobody else drinks tequila that way.

GRETA: There's nothing wrong with being singular.

ASTA: Rules exist for a reason. Without rules all we have is anarchy.

GRETA: You're such a conformist.

ASTA: I'm not a conformist. I just believe that there's an order of things and things should be held to that order.

GRETA: You're a conformist. Look at you. Everything about you screams conformity.

ASTA: Really!

GRETA: Not a thing out of place on you. Even when you're late for something you follow a distinct and quite regular pattern.

ASTA: Shut up and finish your drink.

GRETA: Okay.

Greta sips.

GRETA: This isn't really a good sipping tequila.

ASTA: Oh, just give it to me.

Asta takes the tequila and drinks the rest of it in one gulp.

ASTA: There. Now let's get out of here and solve some crimes.

Greta and Asta get up and walk away as Jimmy, an itinerant citrus salesman, enters.
He walks up to the Bartender.

BARTENDER: What'll it be, Jimmy?

JIMMY: Orange juice, twist of lime.

BARTENDER: Easy there, big spender. You sure you don't want something stronger?

JIMMY: You're right. Give me a couple more slices of lime.

BARTENDER: Whatever you say, Jimmy. I just thought you could use something a little stronger.

JIMMY: I asked for more lime, didn't I?

BARTENDER: Yes, you did. I stand corrected.

JIMMY: You know what's wrong with people?

BARTENDER: I'm sure I don't.

JIMMY: People suck. Most people just suck a little here and there, but then there are people who suck a lot and hard. This is good orange juice.

BARTENDER: It's fresh squeezed.

JIMMY: And those people—

BARTENDER: The ones who suck a lot and hard.

JIMMY: Yeah, they really make life difficult for people who are trying hard not to suck.
You take something simple, like love—

BARTENDER: You think love is simple?

JIMMY: It should be. It would be if so many people didn't suck or if everyone sucked about the same. But you get these people who suck because they don't understand that attraction isn't about logic and that's why you can't trust attraction. But then you can't logic your way into a relationship. Did you use key limes?

BARTENDER: No, they were regular limes.

JIMMY: Good. Now, logic and reason are really good for figuring out who you should be with in a relationship, but like I was saying, you can't logic your way into a relationship because attraction doesn't listen to logic or reason or even common sense.
If it did, then I wouldn't know what it means to do "The Baltimore Dump Truck."

BARTENDER: What's the Baltimore—

JIMMY: I'll tell you later. Now, when faced with this eternal dilemma that you need some logical sense to make a relationship work but that you end up in relationships because of attraction that had nothing to do with a plan, people who don't suck or who suck as little as possible give themselves up to the paradox. Because there's no formula that can really fix this paradox. You're attracted to someone for reasons that don't always mesh with the reasons you want to be in a relationship with someone. In fact, sometimes you find yourself attracted to someone who is absolutely wrong for you. Sometimes you crush the heart of a perfectly nice person because you reject them because you're too busy chasing after a very attractive meth addict who proceeds to destroy your life. But here's where people really suck…because they think they can avoid this destruction by establishing rules. And these people with rules, they're the ones that suck the hardest and the most often, because they think that they can control who they end up with in a relationship because they swear they're only going to be attracted to certain qualities, but what they don't realize is that sometimes fate is a trickster that sometimes likes to smother your private parts with wilted jalapenos and then set fire to your car—No, that's not "The Baltimore Dump Truck."—and all your rules of attraction did nothing to keep your car or your junk from burning. And that's why people suck so much. Well, it's one of the big reasons.

During the above rant ABBA have appeared from behind the bar and they proceed to strangle the bartender. Jimmy does not notice this no matter how long it takes.

ANNI-FRID: That makes a lot of sense.

JIMMY: Thanks.

Pause. Jimmy salutes ABBA with his drink.

JIMMY: This is really good orange juice.

Lights.

7. ABBAPHOBIA

The hotel room. The Abbaphobe stands in a spotlight.

ABBAPHOBE: Fear is a real thing. I wake up every morning with an interminable fear. It is a universal fear and a very specific fear. Everybody is afraid to die. Every one of us thinks about death and how it will sooner or later come for us. You're thinking about it right now. You're doing your best to not think about it, but it's in your head now. But in your head it's probably just an abstraction. It's still not real for you. You're running through all the ways you could die and there are just so many of them that you might as well not worry about the specifics. You can't decide between being afraid of being hit in the head with a flank steak or being bitten by a raccoon with syphilis.

But my fear is tangible. My fear is calculable. Because for many years now I've been afraid of being killed by ABBA.

I have imagined them coming to me in the night, sequins glittering in the moonlight, their shiny daggers cutting me to pieces with their infectious rhythm.

I have imagined them riddling me with bullets, drowning me in butter and snapping my head open like a PEZ dispenser.

I imagine them now chasing me around the parking lot of a Holiday Inn near Providence, Rhode Island.

They are like Swedish cheetahs.

I try to run, but my legs won't move.

I try to scream, but my voice is silent and the only thing I can hear is the detached voices of Benny, Bjorn, Agnetha and Frida as the Swedish pop quartet hunts me down.

It is strange to me that they are ageless.

As if somewhere in my imagination it is forever 1979.

Or really, anytime between 1973 and 1981.

But mostly 1979.

Where does this fear come from?

Where does this irrational fear come from?

I call this fear irrational because it is based on an impossible premise. How could ABBA reunite just to kill me? And if they did reunite, how is it that they haven't aged a day, even though logically they should have and a quick jaunt to the internet shows that they clearly have aged? But my fear is based on an ABBA that no longer exists reuniting just to kill me.

I might as well be afraid of dying from toe fungus. I stand a greater chance of being shot by Phil Spector or choked to death by three of The Four Tops than I do of being murdered by ABBA.

And yet I am afraid. I am afraid of ABBA as surely as some of you are afraid of persimmons.

I have let this fear drive me around the world, never sleeping in the same place twice lest ABBA find me.

In this way I have stayed one step ahead of ABBA.

Unless I've been one step behind the whole time, and all my hiding has been nothing more than marking time until the moment when ABBA strikes.

In which case I might as well have stayed home and waited for ABBA to come to me instead of leading them through every hotel or bed and breakfast in the world.

Tonight I'll eat that mint on the pillow and try to fall into a sleep without dreams.

Maybe ABBA will come for me tonight. Maybe they wont. And tomorrow I'll check out and head for my next destination and go through the same routine again.

One day ABBA will find me.

I'm sure of it. I can't imagine any other alternative.

Lights.

8. ABBA: A BALLET IN TWO SCENES

Music. Something like "Ice Dance" by Paul Reeves.

Dancer 1 enters dancing.
Dancer 2 enters dancing after Dancer 1.
They come together.
They break apart.
They reach for the sky.
They reach for the ground.
They reach for each other but are too far apart to touch.

ABBA enters.
Dancer 1 and Dancer 2 dance away from them in fear.
As in previous scenes, Agnetha and Frida and Benny and Bjorn try to stay at 90° angles to each other at all times. They stalk the Dancers.
There is some stylized dancing.
Dancer 1 is stabbed.
A length of red ribbon represents her wound.
Dancer 1 dances and falls into the arms of Dancer 2.
Dancer 1 dies.
Dancer 2 rises up and attempts to dance his/her way to vengeance.
But Dancer 2 is halted by one of the members of ABBA. The ABBA member looks at Dancer in the eyes briefly (they are in profile to the audience) and then turns Dancer 2's head toward the audience.
Dancer 2 dies, his/her neck snapped. ABBA place black dinner napkins over the faces of the victims and dance off. Music ends.

Music begins again. Asta and Greta open the hotel room door and dance in. They dance toward Dancer 2's body and proceed to propose theories on the means of death through dance. They disagree. They move on to Dancer 1's body and do the same. Greta dances to the minibar and grabs a

Toblerone. *Asta and Greta dance through their nougat-y conflict and dance away from the scene of the crime.*
Music ends.
Lights.

9. THE COOK, THE WAITRESS, THE GAZPACHO AND ITS ADMIRERS

The restaurant/bar area or, if an abundance of space and props permits a change in environment, a kitchen.
Asta is seated across from The Cook.[1] Greta paces with a covered pot.

ASTA: You are the cook, is that right?

COOK: Yes.

ASTA: You made the gazpacho?

COOK: I always make the gazpacho. People really like my gazpacho. It got five stars from a gazpacho blogger who tried it.

ASTA: That must be some gazpacho.

GRETA: It's really good gazpacho.

ASTA: Please don't do that. It's evidence.

GRETA: It's evidence of good gazpacho.

ASTA: We're trying to conduct an investigation here.

GRETA: I like how the garlic doesn't overpower the other tastes.

COOK: Thank you.

---

[1] N.B. In the original production The Cook was portrayed by a woman dressed in a headscarf and otherwise wearing black pants and shirt and an apron. All pronouns referring to The Cook were feminized.

ASTA: Did you know the waitress?

COOK: I suppose.

ASTA: That was a yes or no question.

COOK: I knew the waitress, but you never really know a person.

ASTA: Did you have a relationship with the waitress?

COOK: I was a cook and she was a waitress. That was our relationship.

GRETA: Did you use whole olives in this?

COOK: You have good taste.

ASTA: Who taught you to make gazpacho?

COOK: I taught myself.

ASTA: You're sure it wasn't the waitress?

COOK: If she could make gazpacho she would have been a cook.

GRETA: You can't argue with his logic…or his gazpacho.

ASTA: Stop eating the evidence. You're not from here, are you?

COOK: Nobody's from here.

ASTA: Would you say you fit in here? Would you rather be somewhere else?

COOK: I like it here.

ASTA: If I look at your phone records, what will I find?

COOK: Phone calls to people I know.

ASTA: When did you notice that the waitress was missing?

COOK: I didn't. I came to work. I made the gazpacho.
I took a break. I never saw her.

ASTA: And when did you notice the waitress's head in your gazpacho?

COOK: When I took the gazpacho out of the refrigerator.
I opened up the top and there she was.

ASTA: And you don't know why anyone would want to kill her?

GRETA: I think he's been pretty clear about that.

ASTA: Whose side are you on?

GRETA: I didn't realize we were taking sides. I thought we were conducting an investigation.

ASTA: You're saying you taught yourself to make gazpacho. Why would you do that?

COOK: Because I thought it would be a nice thing to learn.

ASTA: And it's not unusual for someone like you to learn to make gazpacho.

COOK: I like to learn things. I'm curious.

ASTA: And you're not curious about what it's like to decapitate someone?

COOK: Not really.

ASTA: Why not? Is it because you've already done it before? Do you find that boring?

COOK: No! I've never cut anyone's head off.

GRETA: I don't think curiosity about gazpacho leads to murder.

ASTA: I don't care what you think. Did the waitress like your gazpacho?

COOK: Everybody liked my gazpacho. Except for the Norwegian vegans.

ASTA: Would you say these Norwegian vegans had something against you?

COOK: I think they had something against everything. They said the water tasted like pork fat.

ASTA: And so you felt persecuted by the Norwegian vegans?

COOK: Who would make pork fat water? Why would that even be a thing?

GRETA: You're not from here, are you?

COOK: Is anybody ever from here?

ASTA: I wouldn't go anywhere if I were you.

COOK: Where would I go? I have work to do.

ASTA: Don't leave town and don't even think about leaving the country.

COOK: Okay.

GRETA: You'll probably want to get a new pot.

COOK: I'll let the manager know.

ASTA: Remember what I said. We'll be keeping an eye on you. Let us know if you see anything strange.

GRETA: Well, not just anything strange.
Just the murdery kind of strange.

ASTA: Why must you always qualify things I say?

GRETA: I have no idea what you're talking about.

Lights.

10. CAN YOU HEAR THE DRUMS, FERNANDO?

A hotel room. Frida and Not Fernando are sitting up in bed snuggled up together.

ANNI-FRID: Can you hear the drums, Fernando?

NOT FERNANDO: My name's not Fernando.

ANNI-FRID: Can you hear the drums?

NOT FERNANDO: Not really.

ANNI-FRID: They're getting closer now, Fernando. Can you hear them?

NOT FERNANDO: I'm not Fernando.

ANNI-FRID: It's been a long time since we've heard the drums.

NOT FERNANDO: I don't hear any drums.

ANNI-FRID: Can you hear the bugle calls? Can you see the campfires blazing in the night?

NOT FERNANDO: Umm, yeah. If that's what you're into. I can see those fires.

ANNI-FRID: Can you hear the drums, Fernando?

NOT FERNANDO: Yeah, I can hear them now.

Bjorn appears from behind the bed.

NOT FERNANDO: Whoa! I'm not really into that! I don't party like that.

ANNI-FRID: Are you sure you won't change your mind?

Agnetha appears from behind the bed.

NOT FERNANDO: We might be able to work something out.

ANNI-FRID: Can you hear the drums now, Fernando?

NOT FERNANDO: Yeah, sure. I hear them. What's your name?

AGNETHA: You shouldn't lie to Frida.

NOT FERNANDO: Which one of you is Frida?

Benny appears from behind the bed.

BENNY [*cheerfully*]: Hello!

NOT FERNANDO: You're not Frida, are you?

BENNY: No. I'm Benny.

NOT FERNANDO: This party just got weird. I should be going.

ANNI-FRIDA: Stay a while. You won't regret it.

NOT FERNANDO: I'm already regretting it.

AGNETHA: You shouldn't have lied about the drums.

NOT FERNANDO: What is it with you people and the drums? I just wanted some bourbon and maybe a blowjob…from a girl. I didn't ask for a freakshow.

BENNY: Hello.

NOT FERNANDO [*exasperated*]: Hello.

ANNI-FRID: Do you hear the drums, Fernando?

NOT FERNANDO: I'm not Fernando. Ask him!

AGNETHA: Do you hear the drums?

NOT FERNANDO: Yes. No. What do you want me to say?

ANNI-FRID: The truth.

NOT FERNANDO: What truth?

AGNETHA: Pick one.

NOT FERNANDO: This is not turning out how I expected.

BJORN: It never does.

ANNI-FRID: It's a shame. You should have heard the drums.

NOT FERNANDO: Well, this has been a fun party.

ANNI-FRID: It's not over yet.

NOT FERNANDO: It's over for me.

AGNETHA: That is so true.

Benny, Agnetha and Bjorn each produce a weapon.

BENNY: Hello!

NOT FERNANDO: Shit.

Lights.

11. A LITTLE RESPECT

The hotel room. A narrator (either onstage or voice over.)
Henry enters carrying some sort of satchel. Henry looks like
a widget salesman from 1962.

NARRATOR: This is Henry.

Henry smiles at the audience.

NARRATOR: Wave to the audience, Henry.

Henry waves to the audience.

NARRATOR: Henry is a widget salesman. Henry is coming
back to his hotel room after a long day of selling widgets.

Henry nods.

NARRATOR: Henry is really tired.

Henry nods appreciatively.

NARRATOR: And a little hungry.

Henry nods vigorously.

NARRATOR: Maybe Henry should order something from
room service.

Henry clearly thinks this is a good idea. Henry puts down
his satchel and picks up something from nightstand. It's a
Gideons Bible.

NARRATOR: Henry is overwhelmed by the choices in the
menu.

Henry scratches his head as he flips through the book.

NARRATOR: Henry is confused.

Henry nods.

NARRATOR: Henry is reading a bible.

Henry looks up, puzzled and relieved.

NARRATOR: Maybe Henry shouldn't have had those cocktails at the bar.

Henry reluctantly nods.

NARRATOR: Maybe Henry wouldn't be drinking so much if he hadn't been dumped by his girlfriend Lisa a month ago.

Henry looks over at the narrator bitterly and then nods his head slowly in agreement.

NARRATOR: Maybe Henry needs to put down that Bible and pick up the room service menu.

Henry clearly agrees with this.

NARRATOR: Should Henry order the Buffalo Blue Cheese Burger?

Henry nods.

NARRATOR: Or maybe just a Cobb salad?

Henry looks over to the narrator or around to try to locate the voice.

NARRATOR: Or maybe just a Cobb salad?

A knock at the door.

NARRATOR: Who could that be?

Henry shrugs.

NARRATOR: Room service here sure is fast.

Henry nods. Henry goes to open the door. Agnetha is standing there leaning on the doorway seductively.

NARRATOR: It wasn't room service, was it, Henry?

Henry shakes his head.

NARRATOR: Who was it?

Henry shrugs.

NARRATOR: Will Henry invite her in?

Henry is about to invite Agnetha in.

NARRATOR: Or would that be a fatal mistake?

Henry shoots the narrator a dirty look.

NARRATOR: Henry ponders the many bad decisions he's made in his life. He thinks for a moment about his ex-girlfriend Lisa and how much he'd just like to have a moment of happiness again. He also feels a little hungry and is wondering what's taking room service so long to show up with his Cobb salad.

Henry shoots another dirty look at the narrator.

NARRATOR: Or his Buffalo Blue Cheeseburger.
Eventually Henry invites the woman into his room. Does
Henry think this is a good idea?

Henry nods.

NARRATOR: Does Henry *really* think this is a good idea?

Henry hangs his head down and shakes his head.

NARRATOR: Henry doesn't care if this is a good idea, does
he?

Henry shakes his head.

NARRATOR: Henry ponders the situation for a second.
Maybe Henry should offer her something from the mini-bar.

*Henry points to the mini-bar. Agnetha politely declines the
offer.*

NARRATOR: Or maybe Henry should order something from
room service.

Henry picks up the Bible and thumbs through it.

NARRATOR: But what should Henry get?

Henry has an idea.

NARRATOR: Champagne?

Henry nods. There is a knock at the door.

NARRATOR: Boy, service at this hotel sure is fast.

Henry agrees emphatically. He goes to answer the door.
Anni-Frid is standing there.

NARRATOR: That's not champagne, is it?

Henry shakes his head.

NARRATOR: This must be your lucky day, Henry.

Henry nods.

NARRATOR: You have no idea what to do now, do you,
Henry?

Henry shrugs.

NARRATOR: Maybe something from room service?
A little champagne, perhaps?

Henry takes the Bible from Agnetha and sits in between her
and Anni-Frid. There's another knock on the door.

NARRATOR: Maybe the champagne is finally here.

Henry gets up and walks toward the door.

NARRATOR: Or maybe it's a serial killer who will
repeatedly stab Henry in the abdomen until Henry dies a
gruesome death.

Henry shoots a dirty look in the direction of the Narrator.

NARRATOR: But it's probably just room service.

Henry opens the door. Benny stabs Henry. Henry doubles
over and slams the door shut.

NARRATOR: I guess it wasn't the champagne.

Henry is stumbling around in pain.

NARRATOR: At least you only got stabbed once.

Another knock at the door.

NARRATOR: Boy those paramedics sure are fast.

Henry opens the door. Bjorn shoots Henry. Henry slams the door shut and falls to the ground.

NARRATOR: Henry did not see that coming. Maybe he should crawl over to the phone and get some help.

Henry crawls toward the bed where Agnetha and Anni-Frid wave to him encouragingly.

NARRATOR: As Henry crawls towards his impending death—

Henry perks up and looks toward the narrator imploringly.

NARRATOR: As Henry crawls toward what could be either his death or a miraculous recovery he thinks about how nothing he has ever done in his whole life seemed to matter. He thinks about his ex-girlfriend, Lisa, and he can't even muster enough energy to be angry that one of his last thoughts will be about someone who doesn't love him and may never have really loved him.

Henry keeps crawling.

NARRATOR: Henry thinks about how useless it is to have two women in your hotel room when you've been shot and stabbed and your world is shrinking down to a cold and lonely death.

Henry reaches up to Agnetha and Anni-Frid. They look at him piteously for a second and then Agnetha puts down the Bible and grabs Henry's hand while Anni-Frid helps Henry up to the bed where he lies between them in a sort of pieta gesture. Henry shivers.

NARRATOR: Agnetha touches Henry's cold hand and thinks how fragile life is and how nothing you ever do will really matter.
Frida wonders if there's any Toblerone left in the mini-bar.
Henry just feels more and more cold.

Music. Lights fade.

12. LOVE TO HATE YOU

*Lights. The hotel room. Anni-Frid and Benny sit on the bed
(at right angles from each other while a woman lies on the
bed with a pillow over her head. Agnetha and Bjorn,
meanwhile are standing across the room (also at right
angles).*

AGNETHA: I can't believe how racist those Germans were.

BENNY: Racist Germans…I never saw that coming.

AGNETHA: Weren't you surprised?

BENNY: Not really.

AGNETHA: I wasn't expecting it.

ANNI-FRID: I wasn't pleased by it, but I wasn't shocked.
People say nasty things when you catch them with their
masks down.

BJORN: Not everybody is pretending to be someone else all
the time, Frida.

ANNI-FRID: Everyone is pretending. You want to see the
real person, put a knife or a bullet in them and then you'll see
who they really are on the inside.

BENNY: Or you'll just see their insides.

AGNETHA: And those Germans were just a pair of horrific
racists. I didn't believe the kind of language they used.
There wasn't even a call for it. They just came out with it for
no reason. And they seemed like such nice reasonable
people.

BJORN: They always do.

ANNI-FRID: At least they used some really colorful language.

AGNETHA: What does it even mean to call someone a sand-wiper?

BENNY: I think she was saying sand-*viper*.

ANNI-FRID: Sand-wiper would have been more offensive, I would think.

AGNETHA: Still, why would they do that?

BJORN: Remember those college boys from Alabama?

ANNI-FRID: They screamed like children.

BJORN: Remember the filth that came out of their mouths when they started bleeding?

ANNI-FRID: You would have thought they were being killed by the Mills Brothers from what was coming out of their mouths.

AGNETHA: I don't understand how people can live with themselves carrying around so much hate.

BENNY: They don't know any better.

ANNI-FRID: They know. They just don't care.

AGNETHA: I would have never guessed those Germans were carrying such hate in them. They seemed like normal people.

ANNI-FRID: There's nothing like xenophobic hipsters to ruin your day.

BJORN: I think we ruined their day a little too.

BENNY: We can't be sure they were hipsters.

ANNI-FRID: Did you see his pants and her shoes...and those hats? They were German hipsters.

AGNETHA: And really racist.

ANNI-FRID: You have to be taught to hate, but some people catch on to it a little easier than others.

AGNETHA: One minute they're talking about organic guavas and the next minute they're blaming everything on swarthy heathens.

ANNI-FRID: And then they were dead. So there's that at least.

AGNETHA: It's not like we knew who they were beforehand. They might have been perfectly nice people.

ANNI-FRID: You mean like sweet Ramona here?

Ramona attempts to stir. Anni-Frid leans on the pillow a bit.

ANNI-FRID: Come on, Ramona. Don't fight it. Give up the ghost.

BENNY: Would it have made a difference if you had known what kind of person Ramona was?

ANNI-FRID: Is. She's still not quite dead yet.

AGNETHA: I don't know. But those nasty people. If I had known they were capable of such filth I'd have come up with something more interesting for them.

BJORN: What can be more interesting than death? It certainly made them more interesting than when they were talking about gluten-free pancakes.

AGNETHA: I don't mean aesthetically. I mean physically. I would have liked to give them more pain. It was too easy for them to die.

ANNI-FRID: Unlike poor Ramona here who has the lung capacity of a Clydesdale.

BENNY: It's not easy for anyone to die, Agnetha.

AGNETHA: I wanted it to be a bit harder for those Germans.

BJORN: I'm sorry they disappointed you.

AGNETHA: I thought the world had moved on.

ANNI-FRID: You can't bomb all the hate out of people.

BJORN: And seventy years is a long time to go without having some hate bombed out of you.

AGNETHA: This is just depressing me.

ANNI-FRID: At least we got rid of those two.

AGNETHA: It depresses me that they had that within them to begin with.

ANNI-FRID: Every killing is an act of erasure. Whether it's those Germans, those jerks from Alabama who we turned into cat food or Ramona here who is—yes, she's finally dead—whoever it may be when we kill them we erase them from the picture. It's as if they never existed. Whatever they were is erased.

AGNETHA: How many people are out there hiding their real selves, waiting for the right moment to spew that garbage like some sort of filth sprinkler?

ANNI-FRID: The world is full of shitbags and the people who taught them to be shitbags. Now two of them are dead. Erased.

BJORN: You can't kill their hate that easily. It festers.

BENNY: And we're not here to be judges, are we?

AGNETHA: Those people just made me so angry.

ANNI-FRID: And now they're dead. Wiped from the earth. And so is Ramona, who went to her death with a little more dignity and no racism. Are you worried about the moral imbalance there?

AGNETHA: It doesn't seem right.

ANNI-FRID: Maybe Ramona was one of those self-righteous nice people who only act nice in front of people but are secretly judging everyone.

AGNETHA: That's hardly the same as virulent xenophobia.

BJORN: She wasn't all that nice anyway.

Everyone looks at Bjorn.

BJORN: It's true.

ANNI-FRID: I'm trying to make a point here. We're not responsible for the moral results of all of our actions. We were lucky that we managed to kill some really nasty people who might otherwise have continued hiding their hatred in the darkest recesses of their inner thoughts. But we also kill people just to kill people, like that marine biologist.

BJORN: She wasn't very nice either.

BENNY: Bjorn's right. She was really rude to the hostess.

AGNETHA: We also killed the hostess.

ANNI-FRID: It was a busy weekend. We killed a lot of people. My point is that we have to take what solace we can in those rare victories and otherwise just not worry about the moral impact we might have otherwise we'll just go crazy.

AGNETHA: Is that what you said to Fernando?

Pause.

ANNI-FRID: You didn't have to say that.

AGNETHA: When people are confronted with death you see who they really are.

ANNI-FRID: You have no right to bring that up.

AGNETHA: I thought we'd moved beyond right or wrong.

ANNI-FRID: You're meaner than you look.

AGNETHA: Frida, I—

ANNI-FRID: I feel every soul we've put an end to, good or bad. Each one is a complete destruction, right or wrong. I carry that with me. Every one of them is a world that has ended.

Ramona moves her legs and struggles a little.

ANNI-FRID: Still not dead! I'll hand it to you, you've got some fight.

BJORN: Listen carefully in case she says something racist.

AGNETHA: I don't think she has anything more to say.

BENNY: She might be thinking something racist.

BJORN: She's probably just thinking "Why don't they shut up and kill me?"

AGNETHA: Don't make fun of me.

BJORN: How is that making fun of you?

AGNETHA: You can be a real jerk.

BENNY: Well, at least we all know who we really are.

ANNI-FRID: Do we?

BENNY: Don't we?

AGNETHA: I wonder if there's any Toblerone left in the mini-bar.

ANNI-FRID: I think I'm going to have some gin. I never have gin.

Ramona stops kicking again.

AGNETHA: Is she finally dead?

ANNI-FRID: We might have to take her head off just to be sure. Lungs like a Clydesdale.

AGNETHA: Better than those Germans. I still hate them.

ANNI-FRID: We can all agree about that. Now let's get some gin and chocolate and relax for a bit while we salute the plucky Ramona and her horse-like lung capacity.

Lights.

13. THANK YOU FOR THE MUZAK

A square of light representing an elevator. Anni-Frid,
Agnetha, Benny and Bjorn stand in the elevator along with
the ABBAphobe. They stand in awkward silence as ABBA
menaces the ABBAphobe. The elevator bell rings and the
ABBAphone makes a hasty exit.
The Pigeon, a hotel guest, enters the elevator and there is a
moment of silent elevator courtesies followed by another
moment of quiet.

PIGEON: I hope none of you are superstitious about having
five people in an elevator.
I used to have a lot of superstitions about elevators. One
time I was stuck in an elevator for twelve minutes during a
blackout. That was scary. But by then I'd gotten help with
my superstitions. I read that Cormac McCarthy book about
the Mayan Calendar and the ancient astronauts and it just
about cured me of the fear of falling in an elevator shaft.
Does anybody want some gum?

AGNETHA: No, thank you.

BJORN: At least she's not racist.

AGNETHA: Shh!

PIGEON: Bless you. I hope nobody's OCD about germs on
elevators. I used to be really bad about that. I was scared to
death of getting chlamydia from touching elevator buttons.
You know what they say, "fool me once, shame on you" and
I didn't want to take any chances.
I once got a killer case of pinkeye from reading an Elmore
Leonard novel and touching my eyes. It was the one with
the detective whose client ends up getting murdered. I never
finished it because of the pinkeye, but if I ever try to read it
again I'm going to use some rubber gloves.

Did any of you read *The Name of the Rose*?

AGNETHA: Yes.

BENNY: Of course.

BJORN: The gloves.

ANNI-FRID: We get it.

PIGEON: Chlamydia is just the worst thing when you're planning a bachelorette party.

AGNETHA: Sure.

ANNI-FRID: Of course.

BENNY: The gloves.

BJORN: We get it.

PIGEON: But now there's really only one fear I haven't gotten past.

AGNETHA: Spiders?

ANNI-FRID: Chickens?

BENNY: Darkness?

BJORN: The gloves?

PIGEON: Choking during sex.

Silence.

PIGEON: Anybody want some gum?

Silence.

PIGEON: There was this one time when I had some bad clams and was about to throw up—

ANNI-FRID: Is this a long story?

PIGEON: Why?

ANNI-FRID: Because we're going to kill you.

PIGEON: What? Why?

BJORN: We don't really want to go into that.

BENNY: The gloves, you know, and all of that.

AGNETHA: Have you ever read *The Long Goodbye*?

PIGEON: I never got into Raymond Chandler.

ANNI-FRID: And now you'll never have to.

Lights.

14. DOWNTON ABBA

Lights. The hotel room.
Sybil and Septimus Sebastian sit sipping Lapsang Souchong
and staring into the stillness.

SYBIL: Septimus.

SEPTIMUS: Yes, Sybil?

Pause.

SYBIL: Nothing.

SEPTIMUS: Oh.

SYBIL: We should have brought the servants with us.

SEPTIMUS: Should we have?

SYBIL: Yes. We should have. What good is a trip without servants?

SEPTIMUS: And where would they sleep? On the couch?

SYBIL: I suppose we might have arranged for rooms for them.

SEPTIMUS: Outrageous.

SYBIL: Still. It might have been a good idea to have servants, for instance, William, the Groundskeeper would have been very handy.

SEPTIMUS: What use would we have for a groundskeeper in a hotel?

SYBIL: William is very…handy.

SEPTIMUS: I'm sure he is.

SYBIL: Are you insinuating something, Septimus?

SEPTIMUS: I wouldn't think of it. I merely agreed that William the Groundskeeper must be…handy.

SYBIL: Yes, quite. How is your tea?

SEPTIMUS: Fragrant.

SYBIL: It's bergamot.

SEPTIMUS: Yes. Quite.

SYBIL: Of course.

Pause.

SYBIL: Perhaps you would have been happier if we had brought along Delphine?

SEPTIMUS: What do you mean by that?

SYBIL: She does tidy things up so well, doesn't she? You do like to keep things tidy, don't you?

SEPTIMUS: Would you like some more tea?

SYBIL: That would be delightful.

SEPTIMUS: I'll ring up room service.

There is a knock at the door. Sybil and Septimus look at the door.

SEPTIMUS: Room service here is amazingly rapid.

SYBIL: And prescient.

Another knock at the door.

SYBIL: We might at least have brought the butler to forestall such an embarrassing situation.

SEPTIMUS: Indeed.

Pause. Another knock at the door.

SYBIL: I suppose someone should answer the door.

SEPTIMUS: Yes. I suppose so.

SYBIL: Septimus?

SEPTIMUS: Yes?

SYBIL: Do be a dear and answer the door.

SEPTIMUS: I suppose I will.

Septimus gets up officiously and walks toward the door with exaggerated ceremony and sweepingly opens the door where Agnetha, Anni-Frid, Benny and Bjorn are crowded in the doorway.

ABBA: HELLO!

SYBIL: Is it room service?

SEPTIMUS: No.

SYBIL: Then who is it, Septimus?

SEPTIMUS: Several Swedes, Sybil.

SYBIL: Are you sure they're Swedes?

SEPTIMUS: Quite.

SYBIL: I suppose they've come here looking for some sort of ritual sex orgy.

SEPTIMUS: Do you think so?

SYBIL: You did say they were Swedes.

SEPTIMUS: I suppose I did.

SYBIL: Then what else could they be looking for?

AGNETHA: We come for sex orgy, ja?

SEPTIMUS: It appears that you're correct, Sybil.

SYBIL: Do invite them in, Septimus.

SEPTIMUS: Would you care for a spot of tea?

AGNETHA: Tea, ja. Den we make sex pyramid, ja?

SEPTIMUS: Indeed.

Agnetha, Bjorn, Anni-Frid and Benny enter and proceed to take over the tea and pass around the pot and generally upset the prim atmosphere.

SEPTIMUS: At least the numbers are even.

SYBIL: It's a pity. I do like the syncopation that comes with odd numbers.

SEPTIMUS: Sometimes you disgust me, Sybil.

SYBIL: And yet you love it, don't you?

SEPTIMUS: I'm afraid I do.

SYBIL: Shall I unleash Mister Figglesworth on the proceedings?

SEPTIMUS: In front of strangers, Sybil? Some things should remain within the family.

SYBIL: Don't be silly. The Groundskeeper has seen Mister Figglesworth several times since last September.

SEPTIMUS: I would say I'm shocked but I brought Mister Figglesworth out for Delphine when she was tidying up the conservatory last Wednesday...and Thursday.

SYBIL: So you see, Septimus, there's no sense in sequestering Mister Figglesworth when we have several Swedes present.

SEPTIMUS: But William and Delphine are practically part of the family. This is something else entirely.

ANNI-FRID: We make sex pyramid now, ja?

BENNY: We have assembly instructions.

Benny unfolds a piece of paper with some sort of rudimentary line drawings and schematics for what might be construed as either a coffee table or a sex pyramid. Septimus looks at the intructions and passes them along to Sybil whose eyes widen as she looks at the instructions.

SYBIL: Mister Figglesworth will just have to wait. There's no sense holding up the proceedings.

SEPTIMUS: I suppose not. Though I suspect we'll have a deuce of a time with this without a small can of treacle to help bind things.

The six of them proceed to awkwardly arrange themselves and then disengage and look at the instructions and reattempt it. After several unsuccessful arrangements they break up and huddle over the instructions.

SYBIL: What if we get a running start?

AGNETHA: Ja, that is a good idea.

SEPTIMUS: I can start from the balcony with one or two of you and then we can use that momentum to catapult you into position, Sybil.

BJORN: That's a good idea.

BENNY: Let's break on three.

ALL: One, two, three, break!

Septimus, Anni-Frid and Agnetha take up a running position on the balcony. Sybil, Benny and Bjorn take up some sort of receiving position for this strange game of red rover. Music. Just as Septimus is about to run Anni-Frid and Agnetha each pulls out some sort of stabbing instrument. Anni-Frid spins Septimus around and stabs him and then Agnetha spins him around and stabs him again. Then they both push him toward the others.

SEPTIMUS: Sybil.

SYBIL: Yes, Septimus?

SEPTIMUS: It appears as though I've been stabbed.

SYBIL: Oh dear. Was that part of the instructions?

SEPTIMUS: No, I don't suppose it was.

SYBIL: Septimus?

SEPTIMUS: Yes, Sybil?

SYBIL: It appears as though I've been stabbed too.

SEPTIMUS: Oh dear.

A melee proceeds mostly hidden from view behind the bed with the occasional head popping up.
Finally Sybil and Septimus pop up from behind the bed.

SEPTIMUS: Sybil?

SYBIL: Yes, Septimus?

SEPTIMUS: This is a terrible sex orgy.

SYBIL: Septimus?

SEPTIMUS: Yes, Sybil?

SYBIL: I'll admit that I find it strangely satisfying.

Lights.

15. THE SEVENTH SAMURAI

Lights. Music. Something almost recognizable as an ABBA melody but in a Japanese style. Tomoe, a samurai, sits on the floor calmly pouring a cup of tea. Her retainer stands guard behind her.

TOMOE: Snow falls on Fuji's peak
        Cherries bloom in Mariko's garden
        The pebble falls into the pond
        But the ocean is still

        The four winds are born
        Of the same breath
        But each blows against the other

        The horse has no rider
        The leaf has no tree
        The end has no beginning
        The I has no me

Benny, Bjorn, Agnetha and Anni-Frid enter. Each is armed in some sort of fashion.

TOMOE: The sun sets
        The moon rises
        The frog jumps
        The storm arrives

ANNI-FRID: The eagle flies high
        The hour is late

What follows is less combat and more of a symbolic series of movement representing combat as Anni-Frid, Agnetha, Benny and Bjorn each fight the retainer.

TOMOE: I knew this day would come.

AGNETHA: And yet you still resist.

TOMOE: The will to live is strong, even with those prepared to die.

THE RETAINER: I'm not really prepared to die.

TOMOE: That's what makes you such an effective retainer.

There is some more combat. The retainer is mortally wounded.

THE RETAINER: I am wounded to death.

TOMOE: We are all wounded to death.

THE RETAINER: But me first.

The Retainer dies.

TOMOE: The end of the magic is the beginning of life

ANNI-FRID: And the end of life is the beginning of the magic

TOMOE: All the oceans are the same water
        Each drop returns to the whole

Anni-Frid, Agnetha, Benny and Bjorn surround Tomoe and then they simultaneously lift their weapons in the air to strike. Blackout.

16. MONEY, MONEY, MONEY

Lights. The hotel room. Agnetha, Bjorn, Benny and Anni-Frid sit on the bed as Tony Romo, a slick motivational speaker holds forth. (N.B. Tony Romo can be played by a woman or a man or any other variation thereof.)

ROMO: I want to congratulate you for taking the first step on your way to optimizing your success.

BENNY: Thanks, Tony.

ROMO: Optimizing success is not about working hard. It's about working smart.
You have to maximize your connectivity in order to expand your financial possibility.

BENNY: That's great, Tony.

ROMO: Think about how many opportunities for optimizing your income you've let slip through your fingers.

Pause.

ROMO: Are you thinking about it?

AGNETHA: Three.

ROMO: What?

AGNETHA: I've let three opportunities for optimizing my income slip through my fingers.

ROMO: Oh. I didn't mean that you should—

ANNI-FRID: Five.

ROMO: It's not a literal—

ANNI-FRID: And a half.

AGNETHA: It's not a competition.

BENNY: Actually it is.

ROMO: No, it's not.

BJORN: Benny's right. You said that in order to find the pathway to success we have to open up our competitive box…or something like that.

ROMO: I never called it a competitive box.

ANNI-FRID: I found it to be an incredibly offensive term.

AGNETHA: I thought it was mildly empowering.

ROMO: My point was that if you want to optimize your income capitulation you have to start with a plan.

ANNI-FRID: You want us to capitulate our income?

ROMO: Don't you want to optimize your success?

BJORN: Why else would we be here?

Pause. Everyone looks at each other.

ROMO: Think about the root of the word. Capitulate comes from capital. You know what capital is?

BENNY: Yes. I do.

ROMO: When you capitulate your income your success grows but only if you believe in your success.

ANNI-FRID: So it's by faith alone that we'll get rich?

AGNETHA: Faith and a competitive box, apparently.

ROMO: I didn't really say that.

BENNY: Are you saying that belief has nothing to do with faith?

BJORN: I hope not. Because that would be incredibly stupid.

ROMO: What? I just said that you have to believe in your success in order to be successful.

ANNI-FRID: That seems fair. But what about death?

ROMO: Death? If you're optimizing your income you really have to put aside negative words.

AGNETHA: So, you don't think about death?

ROMO: This isn't really about me.

ANNI-FRID: Oh, but it is. Do you believe in death?

ROMO: I don't understand what you mean.

ANNI-FRID: It's a simple question. Do you believe in death?

ROMO: I think we're getting off topic. You have to concentrate on your desire to grow yourself with personal success.

BJORN: How much money would you trade to avoid death?

ROMO: That's not how things work. If you believe in your success then you can just—

Bjorn pulls a pistol out and points it at Tony Romo.

BJORN: That wasn't a rhetorical question.
How much money would you trade for your life?

ROMO: Listen, you won't get away with robbing me. I have powerful friends—

ANNI-FRID: Who aren't here.

ROMO: We can work something out. There's no need to be desperate.

BENNY: You seem very desperate to believe that.

ROMO: I have a lot of money.

AGNETHA: Oh, we know. That's why we're here.

BENNY: It's not because we like your shoes.

ROMO: What's wrong with my shoes?

ANNI-FRID: I wouldn't be caught dead in them.

Anni-Frid stabs Tony Romo in the back. Tony Romo sinks slowly to the ground.

ANNI-FRID: I want you to remember this. The last thing that anyone had to say to you right before you died was that they wouldn't be caught dead in your shoes.

AGNETHA: It's okay, Tony Romo, we'll remember it for you.

Tony Romo dies. Lights.

17. DANCING QUEEN

Lights. The hotel room. Asta and Greta are holding up a sheet while looking at some sort of jumble on the bed.

GRETA: How can we even be sure that's just one person?

ASTA: Actually, it's not. Unless it was someone with fifteen toes.

GRETA: I'm going to be sick.

ASTA: Of course you are. You've been eating too much nougat.

GRETA: It's not the nougat. It's the jumble of dead spring breakers.

ASTA: It's the nougat. That stuff is not meant to be consumed in large quantities over a consistent period of time. I'm not sure how you even manage to have bowel movements anymore.

GRETA: I'm touched that you've taken an interest in my evacuations.

ASTA: There were three in the bathroom.

GRETA: Well, that's just sick.

ASTA: No, not that. There were three bodies in the bathroom.

GRETA: I hate myself for thinking that's less sick than three piles of shit.

ASTA: The girl in the bathtub was only seventeen.

GRETA: Did you count her bone rings?

ASTA: She was wearing a t-shirt that had "Only Seventeen" written on it.

GRETA: That's not exactly evidence.

ASTA: Also, her driver's license was next to the sink.

GRETA: Did she still have her head?

ASTA: Surprisingly enough, they left her head.

GRETA: Attached?

ASTA: Mostly.

Pause.

GRETA: Well, they had some party in here before things took a turn. There's not a thing left in the minibar.

ASTA: They literally made mincemeat of the six people in the bed.

GRETA: Six?

Asta lifts the sheet.

ASTA: At least. Unless you know someone who's got three of those.

GRETA: No, but I know two who have only one.

ASTA: That's why I said "at least six."

GRETA: They must have some toolbox to pull this off.

ASTA: And the noise from the party covered all the noise from the slashing and chopping and screaming and dying.

GRETA: Are we in the same hotel?

ASTA: Why do you keep asking that?

GRETA: They all look alike. Every place looks like the last one. I don't even remember where we are anymore.

ASTA: Every hotel is about the same.

GRETA: But it would be profoundly unlucky if all of these were happening in the same place.

ASTA: It's profoundly unlucky wherever it's happening.

GRETA: I wonder why they left her head.

ASTA: They're inconsistent. Sometimes they take the heads, sometimes they put them in gazpacho, sometimes they leave them attached...mostly. You can't expect logic from killers.

GRETA: I'm not looking for logic, just a pattern. Why did they let the party go on so long? Or was the party in progress when they came in? Or did the party start when they killing started? Why did they take the room service menu but leave the Bible behind?

ASTA: They weren't spiritually hungry.

GRETA: Are you getting a sense of humor?

ASTA: I picked one up from the gift shop.

GRETA: Maybe they are spiritually hungry, but just can't be satisfied by what they've found.

ASTA: That's a fascinating psychological insight, but it doesn't help us find our killers or killer.

GRETA: You still think one person can do all of this?

ASTA: I'm not ruling anything out.

GRETA: All this destruction, just to take out a party. It's like something out of Beowulf.

ASTA: So now you think Grendel did it?

GRETA: Or Grendel's mom. Think about it. Grendel can't stand the noise from Hrothgar's party. It drives him mad. He comes up and slaughters the partiers. What we have here is a Grendel or Grendel's mother responding to the noise that drives them into a killing rage. It would explain the viciousness of the killings. Once the quiet returns they slink back into their room again.

ASTA: That's an interesting theory for this murder. It doesn't explain the others.

GRETA: But what if this Grendel effect is metaphorical?

ASTA: I don't like where this is going.

GRETA: What if this Grendel responds to all kinds of stimuli in the same way? What if our Grendel sees everyone as if they're Hrothgar's companions making noise that drives him mad? And then Grendel kills until the noise is gone. But the noise is never gone because there's still more people to kill.

ASTA: And this is all a metaphor?

GRETA: Something about the people, something about the culture, something about the world is triggering this Grendel to destroy everything. Some sort of metaphorical noise of culture is making this metaphorical Grendel go on a killing spree until the noise is gone.

ASTA: Or until Beowulf shows up and chokes him to death and his mom, too, just to be sure.

GRETA: It's just a theory, more of a structural hypothesis, really.

ASTA: I'm sure it'll look good in a book.

GRETA: Thank you.

ASTA: In the meantime we have to find Grendel or Grendel's mom and stop him or them or it or its mom.

GRETA: Right. Where do we start?

ASTA: We might as well start with the room directly underneath this one.

Lights.

18. KNOWING ME, KNOWING YOU

Lights. The hotel room. Agnetha, Bjorn, Benny and Anni-Frid move around in completely non-realistic combinations as if walking through the choreography for a music video during the whole scene.

AGNETHA: I'm concerned about the sexualization of our violence.

BJORN: You think there's something inherently sexual about killing people in hotels?

AGNETHA: No, I was worried about the gender issues.

BJORN: You think there's something inherently sexist about killing people?

AGNETHA: I worry about the message it sends.

BENNY: I think the message it sends is pretty clear.

ANNI-FRID: Didn't we have this same discussion at the last hotel?

BENNY: Aren't we in the same hotel?

AGNETHA: They all look alike. It's always the same smell.

BJORN: I used to be able to feel the difference in the towels. Now I'm not so sure anymore.

AGNETHA: I don't like killing people in a way that glorifies the sexualization of death.

ANNI-FRID: Death doesn't care about anyone's genitals or their gender identification.

BJORN: I'm not sure how we would go about killing people in a way that removes any possible interpretations in the eye of the beholder.

AGNETHA: So you think it's completely subjective if we stab a girl and cut her head off?

BJORN: I don't know what kind of objective meaning there would be to that.

BENNY: Objectively speaking, the girl would be dead.

ANNI-FRID: And headless.

AGNETHA: I think we should be more careful about what message we send with who we kill and how we kill them.

ANNI-FRID: Seriously, didn't we already have this same discussion at another hotel, or maybe even this one?

BJORN: Who is our audience? Who cares? I know you. You don't really care either.

AGNETHA: You have no idea who I am or what I think.

BENNY: Uh oh. Trouble in paradise.

ANNI-FRID: You think this is paradise?

BJORN: Don't get upset.

AGNETHA: Don't tell me what to do or to think. You don't know me.

ANNI-FRID: Nobody knows anybody.

BENNY: Thanks.

ANNI-FRID: Everything isn't about you.

BENNY: No, nothing is about me.

AGNETHA: Maybe it would be better if we went our separate ways.

ANNI-FRID: Haven't we already been through this before?

BJORN: A thousand times. Maybe this time it's the right time.

AGNETHA: You don't know what's in my mind. You nod and smile and pretend to listen but you don't really listen or care, much less understand. You don't actually respect me, not because you don't want to and not because you don't love me, but because you don't know how. Maybe it would be better if we were alone.

ANNI-FRID: We're all alone anyhow.

AGNETHA: Yeah, but me first.

Pause.

BJORN: It would be stupid to fall apart just when we figured out what we have to do to keep us together.

AGNETHA: What *we* have to do? You mean what you have to do.

BJORN: You teach me. I learn. I understand. I listen. Seriously.

ANNI-FRID: On the other hand there's a lot to be said for being alone.

BENNY: Thanks.

ANNI-FRID: You're welcome.

AGNETHA: Now that I think about it I think maybe we did already have this exact same discussion before.

BJORN: How did it end the other time?

AGNETHA: I'm not sure it did.

Lights.

19. TAKE A CHANCE ON ME

*Lights. Music. Something like Daniel Johnston's "True
Love Will Find You in the End" or Okkervil River's "Lost
Coastlines" or maybe something completely different like
some sort of doo-wop tune.*
Lena and Werther sit in chairs facing the audience.
Each has a small table/desk in front of them.
*Lena has a bottle of pills in front of her. Werther has a pistol
in front of him.*
Each looks down at their respective instruments of death.
They look back up.
*While they stare straight out at the audience Benny and Anni-
Frid take the pistol from Werther's desk and replace it with a
bunch of flowers while Bjorn and Agnetha replace Lena's
bottle of pills with a bottle of gummy vitamins or a giant size
Toblerone bar.*
Werther and Lena look down. They look up.
*Werther produces a bottle of poison. Lena pulls out a
straight razor. They look down. They look up.*
*While Werner and Lena look at the audience Benny and
Anni-Frid replace Werther's poison with a glass of water
and Bjorn and Agnetha replace Lena's razor with a vase.*
*Werther and Lena look down, they look up. They each
produce a length of rope.*
*Werther and Lena get up from their chairs and try to toss
their ropes in the air to hang themselves.*
*On the second attempt Benny and Anni-Frid take Werther's
rope and Bjorn and Agnetha take Lena's rope.*
They replace the rope with copies of Boris Pasternak's
Doctor Zhivago.
*Werther and Lena each get up picking up what's on their
respective tables.*
*They turn and for the first time Werther and Lena notice each
other.*
They notice each other's copies of **Doctor Zhivago**.
Werther gives Lena the glass of water and Lena gives

Werther the vase.
Werther puts the flowers in the vase. Lena pours a little
water in there.
They take a step toward each other.

Lights fade out.

20. ABBATOIR

Lights. Anni-Frid, Benny, Bjorn and Agnetha are tied up and seated on the bed in the hotel room. Matamoros stands menacingly across from them with a cordless power drill, clearly in control of the situation.

MATAMOROS: You can go ahead and scream as much as you want. I've taken care of the sound issues.

AGNETHA: Why would we scream?

MATAMOROS: If you knew what I was going to do with you, you would never stop screaming.

ANNI-FRID: Are you going to cut us open and then sexually violate our gall bladders while we watch?

MATAMOROS: What?

ANNI-FRID: Or are you going to make hats out of our genitals and put on a flesh haberdashery fashion show?

MATAMOROS: If you think these amateur theatrics are going to impress me, then you're sadly mistaken. I know it's all false bravado.

AGNETHA: You have no idea who we are.

BJORN: It's true. We barely know each other and we know each other intimately.

MATAMOROS: Oh, we're going to get to know each other real well. When you come face to face with death I'll see who you really are.

ANNI-FRID: Do you think you're going to find Beowulf or Grendel?

MATAMOROS: I'm not really a fan of books.

BENNY: That's a pity. There are a lot of fine things hidden in books.

MATAMOROS: I'll admit that you people are making this so much more interesting than I'm used to. Usually people are like cattle. They don't have much to say unless you drag it out of them and even then it's just such a jumble. But you people are better than the average spring break slumber party massacre. It's going to be a real pleasure doing terrible things to you.

ANNI-FRID: Likewise.

MATAMOROS: What?

AGNETHA: Did you go to clown college?

MATAMOROS: No.

AGNETHA: Do you have any special skills?

MATAMOROS: This isn't a game show. My special skill is that I'm going to murder you all. Sometime before that I'm going to do some unspeakable things to you.

ANNI-FRID: Are they unspeakable because you're inarticulate?

AGNETHA: If you can think it you might as well be able to speak it.

MATAMOROS: You're trying to get me angry but it won't work. I'm not going to make this easy on you.

ANNI-FRID: I prefer it hard.

MATAMOROS: Do you realize who I am?

ANNI-FRID: You're Achilles and Hector and Polyphemos the Cyclops.

AGNETHA: You're Beowulf and Grendel.

MATAMOROS: I'm the one who's going to drill holes in all your bones until I know everything there is to know about you. You're weak. You need to be put in your place.

ANNI-FRID: Let's go ahead and finish this.

Anni-Frid breaks free of her bonds and pulls out a knife. The rest do the same.

AGNETHA: You were saying…

MATAMOROS: This is unexpected.

BJORN: I was expecting a more thorough pat down.

Bjorn produces a long weapon such as a katana or a baseball bat.

MATAMOROS: I'm sure we can come to an understanding.

AGNETHA: I don't think you have what it takes to come to an understanding.

Benny and Bjorn administer a quick set of savage blows that make Matamoros crumple.

AGNETHA: Some people are just so unimaginative.

ANNI-FRID: Save the head for me.

Lights

21. ALL THAT SHE WANTS

Lights. The hotel room. There's a sense of stars in the sky, perhaps from a disco ball. Anni-Frid and Fernando are lying in bed.

ANNI-FRID: Do you hear the drums, Fernando?

FERNANDO: I do.

ANNI-FRID: I can hear them in the distance and the sounds of the bugles from afar.

FERNANDO: I know. We don't have much longer.

ANNI-FRID: Our minutes will be hours.

FERNANDO: Can you hear the drums, Frida?

ANNI-FRID: I can hear them.

FERNANDO: There's no need to be afraid.

ANNI-FRID: They're getting closer now, Fernando.

FERNANDO: The minutes will become minutes again soon.

Silence.

FERNANDO: Tell me what's wrong.

ANNI-FRID: Nothing.

FERNANDO: Tomorrow I cross the Rio Grande and the fight for freedom and liberty begins.

ANNI-FRID: Those are just words, Fernando. Dreams.

FERNANDO: Yes. And by speaking them we begin the process of making them real.

ANNI-FRID: I wish I could believe that, Fernando.

FERNANDO: Someday it will be true.

ANNI-FRID: Maybe one day when we're old and grey and we don't need to carry our rifles anymore then those words will be true.

FERNANDO: It has to start somewhere.
Do you hear the drums?

ANNI-FRID: I do.

FERNANDO: I must go.

Fernando gets up and leaves. As he does so the lights change and Benny, Bjorn and Agnetha enter.

AGNETHA: You didn't murder him, Frida.

ANNI-FRID: I did. Here. I let him go. That was the same as killing him.

BENNY: It's not the same.

ANNI-FRID: It might as well be.
He walked away and I never saw him again.
The world never changed. And for what?
Every sacrifice was for nothing.
I let my chance at happiness slip away into the night and across the river and all I have is a life full of regrets for things I never did, for people I never kept close to me.
I should have crossed that river, too.

Then maybe something would have changed.
I would have liked to have seen that.

Pause.

AGNETHA: The world did change, Frida. It just didn't get any better.

Lights.

22. SUPER TROUPERS

Lights. The hotel bar. Asta and Greta sit.
In the background Agnetha, Bjorn, Benny and Anni-Frid
dance. Perhaps Jimmy and the ABBAphobe are in the bar as
well.

GRETA: Have we been to this hotel before?

ASTA: Don't start with that again.

GRETA: I'm just saying everything here looks familiar.

ASTA: Including the terrible service. Do we have to get our own drinks?

GRETA: Maybe somebody's been killing off the wait staff.

ASTA: That's not funny. It's probably true.
But it's not funny.

GRETA: You would think they'd have hired more people.

ASTA: It's hard to find good workers these days.

GRETA: Well, the top of the labor market isn't looking to get their heads cut off and floated in gazpacho.

ASTA: Where is that bartender?

GRETA [*looking at ABBA*]: Maybe those people killed the bartender.

ASTA: Those people? They couldn't kill a bottle of vodka.

GRETA: Why not? Anybody can kill.

ASTA: What we have here is a systematic killer. Someone who's driven to kill. Someone who is profoundly different from the rest of us. Those poor people are just the same as us. They're not killers. They're dancers. And not even really that good as dancers.

GRETA: You have no imagination.

ASTA: I have plenty of imagination. I just don't indulge every last bit of it. I keep it to myself.

GRETA: Yeah, right. Do you even have a private life?

ASTA: You have no idea.

GRETA: A couple of slaps and pinches, maybe the occasional electrical shock, but mostly just meatballs and mayonnaise.

ASTA: You underestimate me. I pegged the Deputy Mayor of Glasgow one time in Ibiza.

GRETA: I stand corrected.

ASTA: Best vacation ever. And this was before Ibiza got so filled with hipsters, ravers and hipster ravers. I wouldn't go back now if you paid me.

GRETA: What happened to the Deputy Mayor?

ASTA: It was a vacation thing. You can't take a thing like that too seriously. And there's nothing worse than a clingy Glaswegian.

GRETA: For a second there you were almost human.

ASTA: Listen, Greta, I'm as human as the next person. I just don't need to share everything. And it's not like you're an open book. What do I know about you other than the fact that you're annoying and that you're insides are clogged with nougat?

GRETA: You want to know the real me?

ASTA: Not really. But I feel like you owe me something personal since I shared something personal with you. It's a rule.

GRETA: I like ponies.

ASTA: That's it? You like ponies?

GRETA: And horses. I like them a lot. I've read every novel written about a horse or pony. And I used to want to be a singer. I wanted to win the Eurovision song contest singing about ponies while riding a pony. I gave up my dreams of singing because I wasn't really a great singer and I found that music lessons got in the way of my equine hobbies.

ASTA: Well, that's certainly something.

GRETA: Don't judge me.

ASTA: I'm not judging you.

Pause.

ASTA: Okay, I'm judging you a little. Ponies?

GRETA: We're all living in glass houses. Some of us just hide the glass a little better.

ASTA: Alright. I'll drink to that. IF WE EVER GET SERVED AT THIS PLACE!

GRETA: Seriously, we should just get our own drinks.

ASTA: Alright, but I'm not leaving a tip.

They get up.

GRETA: You really don't think those people could be killers?

ASTA: I just can't see it.

Asta and Greta exit. Lights.

23. MAMMA MIA

Lights. The hotel room. Agnetha and Hubert are in bed.
The door opens and Margot enters furiously.

MARGOT: Aha! I found you!

HUBERT: This is our hotel room. There weren't many places to look.

MARGOT: You're so smug, even though I've caught you and that Swedish chippie.

AGNETHA: I'm not a chippie. I just own my sexual desire.

MARGOT: This marriage is a sham. I'm going back to Melbourne where people don't lie and you can get a good kebab whenever you want.

HUBERT: We can work things out. I still love you, more or less.

MARGOT: Which is it? More or less?

HUBERT: It's a figure of speech, Margot.

MARGOT: Fuck you, Hubert! You're love is a package of lies.

HUBERT: See, that's a figure of speech.

MARGOT: You mean nothing to me now, Hubert.
I can't believe I ever married you.
I hate you and I hate this place.

Benny and Bjorn enter.

BJORN: Are we late for the sex party?

BENNY: Hello!

MARGOT: I told you to wait outside.

HUBERT: Aha! The wombat's shitting on the other side of the fence now.

MARGOT: I don't even know what that means.

HUBERT: It means this marriage is a sham. I'm going back to Sydney where you can get a decent parsnip sandwich. I want a divorce.

MARGOT: Not as much as I want one.

HUBERT: Then I'll give you a divorce. A big fat hard divorce. I'll give it to you over and over again until you're good and divorced.

MARGOT: Give it to me now.

Margot leaps onto Hubert and they begin to make out violently. Anni-Frid enters holding a pistol.

ANNI-FRID: Aha! I found you!

Margot and Hubert break apart suddenly.

ANNI-FRID: This threesome is a sham. I thought we had something special and now I find you here together…with each other. That's just sick.

MARGOT: I can explain.

ANNI-FRID: I've had enough of your lies. How could you do this to me?

HUBERT: We didn't mean to hurt you.

ANNI-FRID: But you did hurt me. And now I'm going to have my revenge.

MARGOT: You wouldn't dare shoot us in front of these witnesses.

Anni-Frid shoots Margot and Hubert.

ANNI-FRID: Actually, I would dare.

HUBERT: I never loved anyone.

Hubert dies.

MARGOT: I should have stayed in Melbourne.

Margot dies.

ANNI-FRID: Who's up for some kebabs?

Agnetha holds up Margot's limp arm. Lights.

24. SOS

Lights. The bar. Anni-Frid and The Captain lean on the bar.

ANNI-FRID: Can you hear the drums, Captain?

CAPTAIN: I can hear the rhythm of your heart beating. You have a strong heart.

ANNI-FRID: You have a nice boat.

CAPTAIN: It's the finest ship afloat.

ANNI-FRID: I don't travel by water very often.

CAPTAIN: There's nothing like a life on the sea. I wouldn't choose any other way of living.

ANNI-FRID: Where would you like to die?

CAPTAIN: On the sea.

ANNI-FRID: That question didn't shock you?

CAPTAIN: I don't shock easy.

ANNI-FRID: You're not another one of those world-weary sea captains are you?

CAPTAIN: No, I'm not weary at all. There's still a new delight to be found in every star up in the sky.

ANNI-FRID: It would be a pity for you to die at sea.

CAPTAIN: Everyone has to die. I'd like to die at sea mostly because I like to live at sea, always going somewhere but never quite content to be anywhere. When you're at sea you are someplace but you're also always on your way. It's the right kind of place for me. It's not for everyone.

ANNI-FRID: I'm going to regret the end of this journey even if I get to where I'm going.

CAPTAIN: I wouldn't worry about it. If it's love, then love will keep us together.

ANNI-FRID: And if it's not love?

CAPTAIN: It will still have been at least a little lovely. Now, if you'll excuse me, I'm going to see what's happened to our bartender.

The Captain exits. Agnetha, Benny and Bjorn pop up from behind the bar.

AGNETHA: There's room on the lifeboat if you want to bring him along.

ANNI-FRID: I think that would ruin the spirit of it, don't you?

BENNY: It's just as well. We'd eventually kill him, too.

ANNI-FRID: Well, everyone has their time. And the Captain's time will be in about five minutes, so we should get to that lifeboat before this ship goes to the bottom.

Pause.

ANNI-FRID: Nobody's going to make a joke about going to the bottom?

AGNETHA: Sometimes you have to let the slow balls go.

Everyone looks at Agnetha.

AGNETHA: You're all sick. Let's get to that lifeboat.

Exit. The ABBAphobe scurries after them wearing a life jacket or life preserver. Lights.

25. THE NAME OF THE GAME

Lights. The hotel room. Agnetha and Bjorn stand at right angles. Benny sits in a chair with some sort of musical instrument. Anni-Frid plays chess on the bed with Death, who is attired in some sort of hooded robe or maybe a hooded sweatshirt.

AGNETHA: After a while everything starts to feel decadent. Even the purity of killing.

BJORN: Maybe we can kill our way out of this boredom.

BENNY: Death isn't the answer for everything.

Everyone looks at Death. Death shrugs.

DEATH: It's true. Your move.

ANNI-FRID: I'll have you yet.

DEATH: Don't count on it. I always win. You're really just playing for time.

ANNI-FRID: Don't get cocky.

BENNY: Does anybody want to split a really big sandwich?

AGNETHA: Room service is so slow since we left them shorthanded.

ANNI-FRID: Have we been in the same hotel all this time?

AGNETHA: Does it really matter? You're playing chess with Death. I don't think we're dealing with reality anymore.

BJORN: Who are we? Where did we come from? Where are we going?

ANNI-FRID: Do you really want to know?

BJORN: No, but if I was curious those would be the questions I would ask.

ANNI-FRID: It's your move.

AGNETHA: What are we doing? Do any of you remember anymore?

ANNI-FRID: We're on the razor's edge here. Hold on to your hats.

AGNETHA: We're not even wearing hats.

BJORN: Were we supposed to be wearing hats?

BENNY: Nobody told me to bring a hat.

AGNETHA: I don't think hats even go with these outfits.

DEATH: Hats are overrated. Your move.

ANNI-FRID: We're bringers of death. Plain and simple. Sometimes that amounts to justice. The rest is…incidental.

AGNETHA: All this moving around and we haven't gone anywhere.

BJORN: It's like we're always on the journey and we never get anywhere.

ANNI-FRID: What did you say?

BJORN: It's like we're always on the journey and we never get anywhere.

ANNI-FRID: We're on the razor's edge. It's your move. Can you hear the drums, Fernando?

Death looks at the board.

DEATH: This is impossible.

ANNI-FRID: Check and mate. Do you hear the drums, Fernando?

DEATH: I never lose.

AGNETHA: It sure looks like you lost this time.

DEATH: I can't believe it.

ANNI-FRID: How about I give you a rematch? Do you like to wrestle?

DEATH: I don't wrestle.

ANNI-FRID: That's a shame. I love to wrestle. I'd love to wrestle with you.

DEATH: I don't see the point in it.

AGNETHA: He must not get his kicks below the waist.

ANNI-FRID: I get my kicks wherever I want them.

DEATH: I don't get kicks at all. It's not in the rules to the game.

ANNI-FRID: Then you should change the name of the game.

DEATH: I still don't see how I could lose.

ANNI-FRID: Believing is everything. Now how about that rematch?

Death shrugs and sets up the board.

ANNI-FRID: Are you sure this is the game you want to play?

DEATH: We're on the razor's edge. I'll try it again.

ANNI-FRID: Rain check on the wrestling?

DEATH: We've got plenty of time.

They continue to play. Lights fade.

26. THE WINNER TAKES IT ALL

Lights. The bar and the hotel room. Greta stands alone in the bar and Anni-Frid is alone in the hotel room.

GRETA: Let's pretend for a moment that life is a musical.

ANNI-FRID: Let's pretend that we're singing a song together.

GRETA: If I could only see you the chase would be over.

ANNI-FRID: Do I want to get caught?
Will that even be the end of me?

GRETA: Let's pretend I can see you for what you are.
What will I see?

ANNI-FRID: How can we go on when we don't know what we are or why we do what we do?

GRETA: Let's pretend that there's an audience and that we're singing a song.
Wouldn't that be a dramatic moment?

ANNI-FRID: Let's pretend that there's such a thing as closure and that you can get it in less than five minutes as long as there's a good melody behind it.

GRETA: Let's pretend we can dance and that there's a chorus of disapproval from our peers.

Asta, Fernando and the ABBAphobe enter on Greta's side and Agnetha, Benny and Bjorn enter on Anni-Frid's side. Agnetha is waving a big Swedish flag and Bjorn is carrying a bayoneted rifle.

ASTA: Let's pretend that there are answers and that we can find them.

AGNETHA: Let's pretend that there's a reason for what we do.

BENNY: Let's pretend that we're out of time and out of touch.

BJORN: Let's pretend that I love you.

ANNI-FRID: Nobody would ever believe that.

BJORN: Too true.

ASTA: Find the solution and we can move on to the next problem. That's what we do.

GRETA: Let's pretend for a second that things are easy as that.

ANNI-FRID: Let's pretend that we're in a musical and that everything works out in the end. What do we do then?

GRETA: Let's pretend that we have an answer for it all. Let's pretend that the world is made of clockwork.

ANNI-FRID: Let's pretend that clocks are perfect to begin with.

GRETA: Let's pretend that we're in love.

ANNI-FRID: Really?

GRETA: Why not, as long as we're pretending?

ANNI-FRID: I see your point.
Let's pretend this night can last forever.

GRETA: Let's pretend our souls aren't wounded by life.

ANNI-FRID: Let's pretend we can hear the drums,
Fernando.

GRETA: Let's pretend that you'll take a chance on me.

ANNI-FRID: Let's pretend that we're in a musical and that
there's an audience.

GRETA: And then let's pretend that we're all alone.

Pause. Asta, Benny, Bjorn and Agnetha and the rest leave.

ANNI-FRID: Let's pretend that there's such a thing as love.

GRETA: Let's pretend that we're alone in the world.

Greta exits.

ANNI-FRID: And then let's pretend that's not true.

Lights.

27. WATERLOO

Lights. Asta and Greta in indeterminate space.

ASTA: We're arresting the cook.

GRETA: The cook?! This isn't *The Hunt for Red October.*

ASTA: There's enough evidence to implicate the cook for at least one of the murders.

GRETA: And what about the rest of them? He couldn't have done all of them. It's not even physically possible.
Have we even been in the same hotel this whole time?

ASTA: It was the cook. You know his kind.
They're different from us. They're not from here.

GRETA: Nobody's ever from here.

ASTA: The cook doesn't think like us. The cook just wants to destroy us. We are the noise and the cook is Grendel and sooner or later we have to destroy him and his mother too.

GRETA: It wasn't the cook and you know it.

ASTA: If he wasn't guilty of this then he'd be guilty of something else. They always are. They're not like us.

GRETA: That doesn't make him guilty. And you know better.

ASTA: We're arresting the cook and that's that.

GRETA: I can't let you do that.

Greta draws her sidearm on Asta.

ASTA: Is that what it's come to? Now we have to fight each other?

GRETA: I won't let you do this. It's not right.

ASTA: There is no right here. There's just what we have to do in order to survive.

GRETA: There's always a choice. It's not easy, but there's a choice.

ASTA: It's not a good choice.

GRETA: But we have to try it.

ASTA: You expect me to buy your crackpot theory?

GRETA: It's as good as anything else we've tried.

ASTA: Then what? Am I supposed to actually believe that ABBA was behind this?

GRETA: Not ABBA as we know them but a form of them.

ASTA: Right. Am I supposed to believe that somehow ABBA exists outside of the corporeal bounds of time and space and that they run around as if it's always sometime between 1973 and 1979 and that they murder people in hotels for no clearly discernible reason?

GRETA: I know it's hard to believe.

ASTA: How am I supposed to believe that? Even if I could wrap my head around that where would it leave me? Let's say it's true. Then what we're up against isn't real, it's a figment of the imagination.

We're in Xanadu and they're Olivia Newton-John.

GRETA: I don't think that's what that movie is about.

ASTA: How do you fight an idea? How do you arrest a thought, a notion, a dream? What kind of prison do I have to make to lock up an imagination?

GRETA: I don't know.

ASTA: And that leaves us nowhere. How can we keep going on when we can't even understand where we are and where we're going much less who we're trying to find and why they exist?

Silence.

ASTA: Well, do we have anything even close to an answer?

GRETA: No.

Pause.

GRETA: But at least now you're asking the right questions.

Music. Asta and Greta look around uneasily waiting for some chorus to ride in. The chorus never comes. Lights fade out.

William M. Razavi

William M. Razavi

William Mohammad Razavi was born in Tehran, Iran in 1973, took his first steps at Fort Benning, Georgia and grew up in Texas where he graduated from Trinity University (BA 1995). He went on to earn an MFA in Playwriting from Brandeis University (1997). His play *Making Up For Lost Time* was workshopped at the American Repertory Theatre in Cambridge, Massachusetts and was nominated for an ATAC Globe award in San Antonio. His radio play *Wenceslas Square* was broadcast on WERS in Boston and subsequently declared "dangerous to the image of Radio Free Europe."

His other plays include *Macbeth, The Next-To-Last-Flight of Amelia Earhart, Lusitania, Daedalus's Other Regret, Mavis Davis and the Nighthawks at the Diner, The Private Life of Ernest Hemingway, The Ricky Harrow Pitcher Show, Illuminati* and *Sullivan's Detours.*

He wrote and directed *The Complete Fragments of Menander: Some Assembly Required & The 27 Minute Odyssey* which were performed at the San Antonio Museum of Art in 2008 and 2009 respectively.

His play *The Sign of the Times* was published in *Trickster's Way* in 2009 and performed at the Luminaria Arts Festival 2010.

He is a freelance writer and director whose film and theatre criticism has appeared in the *San Antonio Current* among other publications.

As an actor he has performed in *Slasher* and *Back of the Throat* at Attic Rep and in *What the Butler Saw, All the King's Men* and *Rosencrantz and Guildenstern Are Dead* elsewhere.

An excerpt from his memoir *Turban Cowboy* was published in *Daily Life though World History in Primary Documents* (Greenwood Press, 2009).

In 2010 he debuted short stories for Literary Death Match at the Dallas Museum of Art and Five Things Austin.

In 2005 a high school named for him opened in Aligudarz, Iran.

He is a co-founder of the Southwest Association of Literary and Dramatic Artists and is the Artistic Director of the Overtime Theater in San Antonio, Texas.

William M. Razavi

58098447R00077

Made in the USA
Charleston, SC
01 July 2016